The Suffolk Coast

THE SUFFOLK COAST

Jon Gibbs

FRANCES LINCOLN LIMITED

PUBLISHERS

To my family for their love and support.

Frances Lincoln Ltd
4 Torriano Mews
Torriano Avenue
London NW5 2RZ
www.franceslincoln.com

The Suffolk Coast
Copyright © Frances Lincoln Ltd 2011
Text and photographs copyright © Jon Gibbs 2011

First Frances Lincoln edition 2011

A catalogue record for this book is available from the British Library.

ISBN 978-0-7112-3080-4

Printed and bound in Singapore

HALF TITLE Great Yarmouth.

TITLE PAGE Happisburgh.

ABOVE, LEFT TO RIGHT: Corton, Corton Cliffs, Kessingland, Walberswick.

CONTENTS

INTRODUCTION

Despite its relatively short length of approximately 47 miles, the Suffolk Coast has plenty of variation in coastal landscape. From nature reserves to areas steeped in wartime history, from traditional seaside towns and villages to the heaviest of industry, the Suffolk Coast provides wonderful subject matter for the landscape photographer.

Until fairly recently I had visited only a handful of places along the coast, so in many ways photographing this book has enabled me to 'fill in the gaps', so to speak, and introduce myself to more locations that I can return to again in the future.

My journey in this book begins a few miles from my hometown of Great Yarmouth at Corton where the effects of coastal erosion are plain to see. This location is by no means the only one to suffer from erosion on this stretch of coastline. The damaging effects of the sea are all too apparent at places such as Benacre, Covehithe, Dunwich and Bawdsey.

The Suffolk Coast has some lovely seaside towns and villages. Lowestoft and Felixstowe are the largest. Both of these locations have lovely seafronts and as well as being popular holiday destinations they are also centres of industry, Felixstowe being home to the largest container port in the UK.

Southwold and Aldeburgh are simply delightful places. Quintessentially English, they are like time capsules of a bygone era, with their beautiful architecture and simple seaside attractions, and without an amusement arcade to be seen.

The smaller coastal villages such as Walberswick and Orford (to name but two) are also lovely places to visit. It is well worth delving into the history of these coastal settlements. For example, Orford Ness will bring stories of wartime experimentation, while Dunwich will show how a city can be lost to the sea.

Aside from the coastal settlements, there are many nature reserves, possibly the most famous on the coast are at RSPB Minsmere and National Trust Dunwich Heath, whose lovely landscapes of marshes and heathland respectively sit in close proximity to Sizewell Nuclear Power Station.

Another major part of the coastal landscape are the estuaries of the rivers Blyth, Alde (which becomes the Ore), Deben, Orwell and Stour. These areas themselves would provide enough subject matter for a book and warrant further exploration from myself in the future.

The Suffolk Coast is a fragile landscape. Much work is being carried out to protect the coast from the effects of erosion which has shaped this coast for hundreds of years. It is a coast worth protecting, spectacular and dramatic are possibly not the words to describe it but there is a subtle beauty and variation that has made this coast a pleasure for me to explore and photograph.

I hope you enjoy the images.

Jon

LEFT: Pakefield.

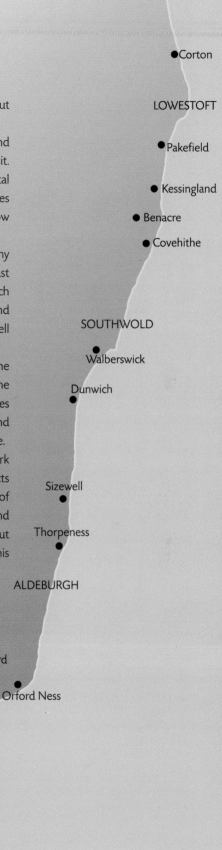

●Corton

LOWESTOFT

● Pakefield

● Kessingland

● Benacre

● Covehithe

SOUTHWOLD

● Walberswick

Dunwich ●

Sizewell ●

Thorpeness ●

ALDEBURGH

Orford ●

● Orford Ness

Shingle Street ●

Bawdsey ●

● Bawdsey Quay

Felixstowe Ferry ●

FELIXSTOWE

CORTON

The sea wall at Corton has become severely damaged and at present a large section of the wall is fenced off due to its dangerous condition. In this image a wave breaks against the wall in dramatic fashion on an April morning.

A view from the top of the cliffs at Corton on a stormy December morning looking northwards towards Gorleston and Great Yarmouth. The wooden sea defences here are in pretty good condition but the unstable nature of the cliffs is all to easy to appreciate judging by the amount of debris at their base.

LOWESTOFT

Sunrise near Ness Point at Lowestoft, which is the most easterly point of the British Isles. The sea defences in this part of Lowestoft are very damaged which makes walking on the beach here very difficult. This area is adjacent to the very large Bird's Eye factory and the industrial hub of Lowestoft.

This picture was taken on the 'Euroscope' at Ness point, which shows distances to other notable points in the British isles and Europe. The 80-metre wind turbine 'Gulliver' is a dominant feature of the local skyline. Beyond the turbine is the Orbis Energy Building, which houses businesses who work in the renewable energy sector.

A calm summer evening at a
busy Lowestoft Marina.

This picture is taken from the South Pier, and shows the view along the beach and promenade. Lowestoft's beach is of a very high standard and regularly wins awards for its cleanliness and water quality.

Early morning in winter on the promenade looking towards the South and North Piers and harbour entrance. The harbour leads to the inland Lake Loathing, which then connects to the Norfolk and Suffolk Broads at the picturesque setting of Oulton Broad.

Sunrise on a winter morning on the South Pier, showing a nearly completed offshore platform.

LEFT Beautiful blueish light showing the sea defences on the main beach with Claremont Pier visible on the right of the image.

ABOVE Sunrise on a midsummer morning showing the silhouette of Claremont Pier. The pier was constructed in 1902–3 and was once over 700 feet long and T-shaped to enable the steamers of the Coast Development Company to berth here.

PAKEFIELD

Dramatic afternoon light bathes the village, illuminating the church of All Saints and St Margaret. On the shingle the fishermen's huts and boats, in very varying conditions of seaworthiness, can be seen.

RIGHT Places like Pakefield are always great locations for photographers. Give a landscape photographer a few old boats and there are enough colours, shapes and weathered surfaces to keep them amused for hours.

FAR RIGHT The old boat winches on the shore make fantastic subjects for abstract studies. There are numerous examples of these on the shingle here.

BELOW A fisherman drags his boat to the top of the shingle on a bright spring morning.

A view of the cliffs looking
southwards towards
Kessingland on a beautiful
July morning.

KESSINGLAND

Subtle colours at dawn, showing a couple of the small number of fishing boats to be found on the shingle at Kessingland. The village is a popular holiday destination and, as well as the usual seaside attractions, the village is home to an African Safari Park.

A brooding sky looms menacingly. Unfortunately, the electrical storm that I hoped would appear failed to materialise, but I was happy with these amazing cloud formations. Some of the lovely properties on the sea wall can be seen in this picture, as well as a couple of caravan sites that are common on this stretch of the Suffolk Coast.

LEFT A summer sunrise over the shingle and grasses in this view looking out towards the North Sea.

RIGHT A shoreline view from a midsummer evening looking back towards Lowestoft.

BENACRE AND COVEHITHE

This picture shows where the cliffs begin to rise again at Benacre, one of the areas most prone to erosion on the Suffolk Coast and, for me, one of the most fascinating place to visit.

One of the features of the
Benacre and Covehithe
area is the number of dead
trees on the clifftops and
on the sand. Their skeletal
shapes make fascinating
photographic subjects.

ABOVE An illustration of this ever-changing part of the Suffolk Coast. It surely will not be long before the tree on the cliff edge falls on to the sand below.

RIGHT The town of Southwold is visible in silhouette in the distance of this picture taken from the shore at Benacre.

A much-photographed
subject, and rightly so. This
tree is very much a symbol of
the area. Here is is being lit
by beautiful late afternoon
light on a cold day in January.

The Benacre and Covehithe area is a very popular location for a seaside walk, but getting down to the beach area is becoming more difficult because of the unstable nature of the cliffs. This picture perfectly illustrates the number of dead trees scattering the area. In the background of the picture is the water of Benacre Broad.

Benacre Broad is part of the Benacre National Nature Reserve, along with nearby Covehithe and Easton Broads. The Broads' proximity to the sea has meant that regular flooding has made them more saline rather than the freshwater state they would have been a few decades ago.

A picture taken beneath the cliffs between Benacre and Covehithe on a stormy October day. At high tide it is impossible to walk along the base of the cliffs for much distance because of the amount of erosion and the soft and slippery nature of the ground at the cliff base. For those wanting to walk further on to Southwold, a walk along the cliff tops is the only option, but this too has its difficulties.

SOUTHWOLD

Southwold is a picturesque seaside town that I love to visit whether as a photographer or taking the family for a day by the seaside. It is full of lovely architecture and has a picturesque seafront dominated by its pier (pictured), lighthouse and beach huts, while in the town there are enough shops, cafés and pubs to while away the hours if the weather is not suitable for a beach-based day.

A beautiful sunrise at Southwold Pier taken on top of the relatively new sea defence boulders that replaced some of the ageing groyne defences.

ABOVE Southwold Pier dates from 1900 and has become an immensely popular attraction in the town since its refurbishment, which began in 1999. Its attractions include shops, cafés and a wonderful under-the-pier show which has some of the most bizarre amusements you are likely to see. Another popular feature is the water clock which attracts many people to see its intricate workings and metal sculptures. In this image the pier is shown amidst a foamy sea on a windy June morning.

RIGHT The rising sun pictured from beneath the pier on a colourful March morning.

LEFT Sunrise on a summer day. At the time of writing the pier was for sale and has planning permission to develop its entrance building (to the left of the image) into a hotel complex.

ABOVE The beach hut is synonymous with Southwold. As a photographer these colourful buildings are the first things I think of when I think of Southwold. It is always interesting to check out their décor and names and see if anyone can think of any new and original names for their huts. Some are far cleverer than others. At the top of the cliff near the centre of the image Southwold Lighthouse is visible. The lighthouse was constructed in the late 1800s and has been automated since 1938.

Beautiful golden light on a
windy morning.

As well as the beach huts there are some rather grand properties on the seafront. Some are visible in this image, taken in beautiful light on a summer morning.

LEFT A view from Gun Hill looking southwards. These 18-pound cannons were allegedly given to the town by the Royal Armouries in the mid-1700s to protect the town. Gun Hill was also the site of the town's original wooden lighthouse.

BELOW LEFT The colourful beach huts on a bright winter day.

BELOW MIDDLE This set of beach huts at the southern end of Southwold beach are probably the most photographed in the town. Perhaps they have just the right variation of colours to keep photographers happy.

BELOW RIGHT A moody spring evening showing a general view looking all the way from the southern end of the beach towards the pier. Southwards from here the beach gives way to the entrance to the River Blyth.

WALBERSWICK

Walberswick is a charming coastal village. Though separated by the River Blyth from the neighbouring Southwold, the two locations are linked by a footbridge across the river. The area around the harbour is a fascinating mix of fishermen's huts and boats of all shapes and sizes. This image, taken on a colourful February morning, shows the harbour wall and sea defences.

Subtle colours at dawn in this
seaward view showing part
of the small area of dunes.

LEFT A crisp September morning on the beach looking southwards towards Dunwich.

BELOW A view on a sunny late summer morning, taken near the harbour entrance. The fishermen's huts that dominate the harbour area on both sides of the Blyth area can be seen here, as well as properties used as holiday accommodation.

The village has long been associated with crabbing and holds its own championships during the summer. The image here, taken on a late summer morning, shows the areas that during the height of summer will be packed with both young and old trying to lure the crabs into their buckets.

LEFT Walberswick has a few beach huts which can rival Southwold for location even if they cannot compete in the colour stakes. They are pictured here on a winter morning as low light creates lovely golden hues in the dunes.

BELOW The small sandy beach at Walberswick gives way to shingle which then dominates the Suffolk Coast all the way to Aldeburgh. This image shows the view towards Dunwich on a stormy June morning.

DUNWICH

A lone boat on the shingle at Dunwich on a very stormy February morning. Dunwich's fame comes from the fact that the village was once a larger town, with great importance as a port and trading centre, but much of the area was lost to the sea in storms and further acts of coastal erosion that began as long ago as the thirteenth century. Today it is a small coastal village and the very few boats on the shingle beach bely its grander past.

THELMA
DUNWICH

RIGHT A study of the boat winches that are used on the very small fleet at Dunwich.

ABOVE Above the beach on top of the crumbling cliffs is the National Trust's Dunwich Heath. This study shows the wonderful colours on show in this mid-August image.

RIGHT Sunrise looking northwards towards Walberswick.

ABOVE Storm clouds bringing
frequent showers move
across the sky as the small
fleet of fishing boats sit atop
the shingle bank, in this
image taken in late spring.

RIGHT A view towards the
National Trust properties
at Dunwich Heath across
the wonderful expanse of
colourful heathland. The
Heath provides wonderful
cliff top views and scenic
woodland and heathland
walks, the colours are at their
best from July to September.

OVERLEAF A bright and windy
spring day on top of the
cliffs near the National
Trust properties looking
northwards with yellow
gorse in full blown.

ABOVE Another view northwards from the cliffs on a much moodier day.

RIGHT Beautiful spring light in this view from the cliffs looking southwards across the marshes of the beautiful RSPB Minsmere Reserve towards Sizewell.

A spring morning view of the
crumbling cliffs and shingle
beach at Dunwich.

Storm clouds pass over on a windy spring morning on the southern end of Dunwich beach.

SIZEWELL

Sizewell Nuclear Power Station dominates the view along the coast for miles. In this image the building that houses the soon-to-be-decommissioned Reactor A is on the left, while the blue building with its distinctive dome houses Reactor B. It is possible that a further reactor will be constructed in the near future. Amid all this modern technology, the village's small fishing fleet sits on the shingle in a typical array of boats, nets and winches.

A dramatic sunrise showing the two power station cooling towers that sit a short distance out to sea.

LEFT A view from the same
dramatic morning as the
previous picture.

ABOVE A view looking
southwards along the shingle
with an old fishing boat
slowly losing its battle with
the elements.

THORPENESS

Rain clouds pass over the crumbling cliffs just north of the village of Thorpeness .In the foreground the remains of wartime defences sit forlornly on the sand.

The cliffs here at Thorpeness
remind me of those at
Benacre. Just north of here
a few properties sit a few
feet back from the cliff edge,
their owners are surely aware
that the sea may reclaim
most of their back gardens
some day soon.

Thorpeness's one and only fishing hut sits on the shingle
adjacent to these lovely seafront properties.

The village of Thorpeness makes a compelling visit. A wealthy Scottish barrister transformed the area in the early 1900s and created a coastal village with mock Tudor and Jacobean architecture. The village also has its own lake and the quirky 'House in the Clouds': a clever piece of architectural disguise that contains a water tower. This image shows these very brightly painted houses that are a dominating presence overlooking the shingle beach.

ALDEBURGH

Suffolk is blessed with some wonderful seaside villages and towns and Aldeburgh is no exception. At the northerly end of its shingle beach is this sculpture called *Scallop* by the artist Maggie Hambling. The work in stainless steel is a tribute to the composer Benjamin Britten and is inscribed with the words 'I hear those voices that will not be drowned', from the opera *Peter Grimes*.

A study of the *Scallop* sculpture. When it was first unveiled it was extremely controversial among the local community, many thought it spoilt the look of the area.

FAR LEFT A general view of the seafront at Aldeburgh on a crisp winter morning, showing some of the small fishing fleet. The architecture and colours of the buildings along the seafront are wonderfully photogenic. The main shopping street in the town is dominated by local independent shops and art galleries and is a lovely place to stroll.

LEFT Studies of fishing regalia on the shingle at Aldeburgh.

LEFT It is possible to buy your fish fresh from the fishermen on the seafront at Aldeburgh. It is fascinating to watch these wonderful characters prepare their catch for sale and one can't help but admire the difficult job they do.

ABOVE A view from the shingle looking northwards on a winter morning.

RIGHT Wispy clouds and clear crisp light mixed with subtly coloured seaside architecture.

The southern end of Aldeburgh beach is protected with wooden groynes and boulders to prevent erosion on the steep shingle beach. This area was once the site of the village of Slaughden, which was a bustling port until the mouth of the River Alde moved further southwards due to erosion. Here the groynes are pictured on a beautiful January morning.

Martello towers were constructed along the east coast in the early 1800s to prevent Napoleon's armies from invading, something that was surely a possibility given the low-lying nature of the coast in Suffolk. This image shows the Martello tower at the southern end of Aldeburgh looking back towards the town.

ORFORD NESS

Along the shingle from Aldeburgh is the spit of land known as Orford Ness, which is in the care of the National Trust. It is a fascinating place that is now a haven for wildlife but its not so distant past as a centre of wartime experimentation means that the wildlife live among the eerie remnants of buildings and land that once were host to top secret work which included testing of atomic weapons. This view shows the lighthouse at Orford Ness, which is deemed at high risk from coastal erosion. There were originally two lights but the 'Low Light' was abandoned in 1887 and has long since gone.

A moody day, befitting of the surroundings. Access to Orford Ness is via a ferry from the village of Orford, rather than from Aldeburgh. Once on the Ness visitors must keep to designated areas as there is still the possibility of unexploded shells being present on the shingle.

The buildings at Orford Ness are scattered over quite a large area and it is fascinating to discover their various uses as you tour the site, though a lot of imagination is needed to try and picture in your mind's eye this place in use.

ORFORD

Orford is a very picturesque village with a stunning castle built in the twelfth century by Henry II. The quiet streets of the village are lined with beautiful period houses and the village has a small harbour with views across to Orford Ness. It is here that the River Alde becomes the River Ore which then flows between the mainland and the spit of Orford Ness before joining with the North Sea near Shingle Street. This image shows the harbour with Orford Ness to the left of the image.

Golden autumnal light on the boats on the shingle at Orford Quay.

LEFT A general view of the harbour. In this image the distinctive Orford Ness lighthouse can be seen to the right of the image.

BELOW Magenta hues in the clouds above Orford Harbour in this view looking across the River Ore. It is also possible to visit the RSPB reserve of Havergate Island from Orford Quay. The small island is a breeding ground for avocets and terns during spring and summer.

RIGHT A beautiful autumn morning at Orford Harbour.

SHINGLE STREET

ABOVE Shingle Street is a small coastal hamlet which has the feeling of being far removed from the rest of the world. It is the location where the River Ore joins the sea and is a popular spot for fishing. This image shows the buildings that would have been fishermen's cottages, this particular building now has a coastguard lookout. This image also shows the painstaking length that someone with an artistic mind has gone to to create a trail along the shingle using shells.

RIGHT A bright August day at Shingle Street. I have never visited here when the weather is particularly rough but I can imagine the area is at some risk from large scale coastal erosion.

Sunset on a beautiful January
day looking southwards.

A view of the entrance to the River Ore showing a beautiful traditional boat entering the river. While watching this scene I was also 'entertained' by a small boat full of fishermen landing on the tiny shingle 'islands' in the centre of the image and fishing them for as long as possible before being picked up and transferred to another to fish there.

A beautiful winter sunset
with shingle, sea and sky.

Wonderful cloud formations over this beautifully sited place. During the Second World War there were rumours that Shingle Street was host to a failed German invasion. This has not been proven, nor has the theory that the reports were an exercise in war propaganda.

BAWDSEY AND BAWDSEY QUAY

Further along the shingle is Bawdsey. This image shows the shingle beach on a bright winter morning looking back towards Shingle Street. This site was also home to a gun battery, whose extensive remains can be viewed beside the car park here. In the distance can be seen one Martello tower that has been developed into a residence. The Martello towers become more of a feature in this part of the Suffolk Coast.

Recently the work has been undertaken on coastal defence schemes. Large granite blocks have been placed on the shingle. These have replaced the older wooden groynes, of which only a few remain, as pictured here along with a pillbox on a moody summer afternoon. Of course the blocks are a necessity but they have far less aesthetic qualities than the wonderfully weathered wooden groynes. Just along the shingle before you reach Bawdsey Quay is Bawdsey Manor, a beautiful stately building used during wartime as a chain radar station.

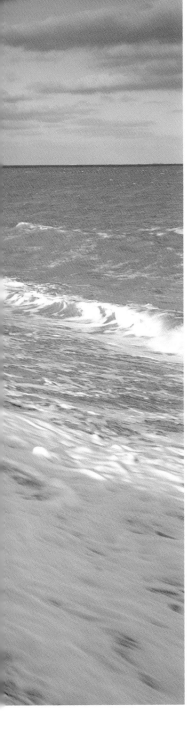

Bawdsey Quay sits on the
entrance to the River Deben
and affords lovely views
across to Old Felixstowe
and inland along the river.
It is pictured here below a
beautiful winter sky.

Looking across towards
Old Felixstowe and the
mouth of the River Deben
from Bawdsey Quay. The
unmistakable outlines of
two Martello towers in Old
Felixstowe can be clearly
seen silhouetted against this
beautiful winter sunset.

ABOVE Warm light at low tide. A ferry crosses from Old Felixstowe to Bawdsey. To the left of the image is the quay where the ferry leaves from.

RIGHT A winter sunset with its beautiful colours reflected in the expanse of mud on show at low tide.

FELIXSTOWE FERRY

The extremes of the boundary of this Suffolk Coast town could not be more different. Felixstowe Ferry, pictured here, is a traditional fishing settlement which sits at the mouth of the River Deben. At the other end of the town is Felixstowe Container Port, the largest in the United Kingdom. This image shows one of the numerous fishing huts at Felixstowe Ferry in the foreground with the River Deben and Bawdsey Quay in the background.

A cold September morning view taken from the pier used by the ferry to Bawdsey.

Wonderful subject matter all around. Felixstowe Ferry has the usual appearance and ambience associated with fishing villages, chaotic surroundings and colourful characters, making this a great place for a photographer to visit.

LEFT Low tide with a subtley coloured sky.

OVERLEAF Studies from Felixstowe Ferry.

The mouth of the River Deben at Felixstowe Ferry showing a Martello tower which has been converted into a residential property. On the horizon are two large container ships heading away from the container port.

FELIXSTOWE

Southwards along the coast from Felixstowe Ferry the main seafront of Old Felixstowe begins. There are literally hundreds of beach huts in Felixstowe, more than I have seen anywhere else on my travels but I wonder if this is the location that has the most examples of these wonderful seaside buildings. In this image the golden light of a late summer morning illuminates the beach huts.

The beach at Old Felixstowe on a windy September morning. This part of the seafront is far more genteel than further along the promenade. In an area of beach known locally as 'The Dip' the remains of a Roman shore fort called Walton Castle can sometimes be viewed among the waves.

A beautiful bright September morning showing beach huts and beautiful seafront properties.

A dawn view along the main part of the promenade. Just behind the beach huts in this image is the concert venue Felixstowe Pavilion. There are beautifully kept gardens lining the promenade here and superb views from the cliffs backing the promenade. In the distance can be seen Felixstowe Pier and beyond that the cranes of the container port.

Pastel shades in both the sky
and on the beach huts on
the promenade.

ABOVE Landguard Point is the southernmost part of the Suffolk Coast at the mouth of the River Orwell. It is home to Landguard Fort, which has in various guises offered protection to this strategically important area since the 1500s. Today it is an English Heritage property. Within this area of heavy industry and ex-military use is a Nature Reserve that is important as a habitat for many rare plants and as a stopover for migrating birds. This view shows Landguard Fort on the right of the image with the container port in the distance.

RIGHT Felixstowe Container Port can accommodate some of the largest container vessels in the world. It brings in approximately 40 per cent of the United Kingdom's import and export trade and deals with roughly 4,000 ships each year. This image is a general view of the port taken from Landguard on a beautiful September morning.

INDEX

A bright winter day at Shingle Street.